I got 99 problems but a stitch ain't one

CROSS-STITCH WITH ATTITUDE

GENEVIEVE BRADING

MITCHELL BEAZLEY

THIS BOOK IS DEDICATED TO EVERYONE WHO THINKS CROSS-STITCH
IS STUCK IN THE PAST. IN YOUR FACE, STEREOTYPES.

An Hachette UK Company
www.hachette.co.uk

First published in Great Britain in 2016
by Mitchell Beazley, a division of
Octopus Publishing Group Ltd
Carmelite House
50 Victoria Embankment
London EC4Y 0DZ
www.octopusbooks.co.uk
www.octopusbooksusa.com

Distributed in the US by
Hachette Book Group
1290 Avenue of the Americas
4th and 5th Floors
New York, NY 10020

Distributed in Canada by
Canadian Manda Group
664 Annette St.
Toronto, Ontario, Canada
M6S 2C8

Commissioning Editor: Joe Cottington
Designer: Jaz Bahra
Additional text: Eithne Farry
Editor: Phoebe Morgan
Photography: Haarala Hamilton
Production Manager: Caroline Alberti

ISBN 978-1-78472-235-7

A CIP catalogue record for this book is
available from the British Library.

CONTENTS

INTRODUCTION

Cross-stitch has been around forever. Those little "X" markings were part of decorative embroidery in the Tang dynasty in China, 1,000 years ago, and after a long and distinguished history finally made their way into your grandma's craft basket, where cute patterns and sweet sayings about "home sweet home" were the order of the day. And for a while it looked like cross-stitching was going the way of sweet sherry – into a bygone age of safeness and nostalgia. That is, until some intrepid crafters realized there was some fun to be had with fabric, a needle and thread, and a mischievous mind. They cottoned on to what your grandma already knew; that there is something very satisfying about kicking back and making stuff.

In the fast-paced, nonstop world that is modern life, it is lovely to just pause, switch off your phone and computer, and do something that is soothing for the soul. Cross-stitch is the perfect craft for this; there's something very calming about pulling the thread through the fabric, and something enticingly hypnotic about repeating the same stitch over and over. And as you have to concentrate it has a way of sidelining stresses and worries so you can focus on the task in hand, plus there's the undeniable glow of creating something from scratch. Nothing can quite beat the pleasure of a completed project – especially if that project happens to be about Beyoncé.

And the particularly good thing about cross-stitching is that it is really easy to do; you can pick it up in an evening, and it won't cost you the earth in supplies. And now, thanks to this very book, there's no risk of you getting bored by following dull patterns that just don't quite do it for you. As you'll see from the 20 patterns in the following pages, the world of cross-stitch has got deliciously rebellious, as this old-fashioned craft takes on the problems of the modern world and emerges as the winner every time.

This book is designed as a beginner's guide to the craft; it's all about getting the maximum enjoyment with the minimum of fuss, so there are no complicated techniques to master – just a few simple-to-grasp steps (shown overleaf) that will set you on your way to stitching projects that will shock, inspire and mildly amuse.

And once you've got the simple skills in hand you can start choosing and making patterns to hang on your wall, or to give as suitably sassy gifts for your friends and family – a world away from the dusty, out-dated needlepoint from grandma's day. Happy stitching.

GENEVIEVE

CROSS-STITCH: THE BASICS

YOUR STITCHING STASH

Cross-stitch doesn't need any heavy machinery or expensive equipment, just a few things from a haberdashery or craft shop:

FABRIC

All of the patterns in this book have been stitched on a fabric called "aida", which is made specifically for cross-stitching. It's woven to create evenly spaced holes that you can stitch through, helping to keep your cross-stitches the same size and level.

Aida comes in different "counts". All of these patterns use antique-white aida, in 14-count, which means it has 14 holes per inch (hpi). The higher the count, the more holes per inch, the smaller your stitches will be.

The pattern size mentioned on each cross-stitch chart tells you how big your work will be if stitched on to 14-count aida. You'll want to cut a piece large enough to fit the pattern plus a border of a few inches, to accommodate an embroidery hoop and help with framing.

EMBROIDERY HOOP

Use an embroidery hoop to keep your fabric taut and your tension even as you stitch. A 22cm (9in) hoop will fit even the biggest project in this book,

meaning you won't need to reposition the hoop as you stitch.

To fit your embroidery hoop, unscrew it and separate the rings. Sandwich your fabric between the inside and outside rings, then, on a flat surface, push the rings back together (1). Tug at the loose fabric all the way round while tightening the screw. Tug, screw, tug, screw, until the fabric is drum-tight. If the screw is stiff, a flat-head screwdriver will be sure to help things along.

When taking a break from stitching, it's best to take your fabric out of the hoop to avoid it leaving marks.

THREAD

Stranded-cotton thread is the go-to thread for cross-stitch. It's made up of six strands and comes wound in "skeins" of 8m (8.7yd). The skeins are bound by paper bands – rather than remove these, pull the thread-tail from the numbered end to unravel it (1). The ideal length of thread to stitch with measures from fingertip to elbow.

Stitch the patterns in this book (or any using 14-count aida) using two strands of thread in your needle, or three for a fuller finish. You could vary your finish from pattern to pattern too, if you prefer.

To separate the strands from one another, pinch the top of the thread firmly. With your other hand, grab hold of a single strand. While still pinching, pull the single strand skyward, fast, (2) until it's free from the others! Straighten the remaining thread for next time.

The colour key on each cross-stitch chart specifies colour codes for DMC-branded thread, a widely available brand. Take these colour codes to a craft shop or haberdashery to buy the right shades of DMC thread with which to stitch the pattern.

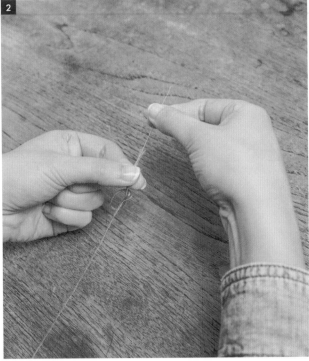

NEEDLE

Tapestry needles are ideal for cross-stitch. They have a large eye and a blunt end that slips through the holes without piercing the fabric. Use a size-24 tapestry needle to stitch onto 14-count aida.

A neat way of threading your needle is to loop your strand-tails over it. Pinch the loop that it creates (3) as you slide the needle out. Then thread it by wiggling the eye of the needle down over the loop (4). Ta-da!

SCISSORS

Embroidery scissors have small, sharp points; they're brilliant for snipping fiddly threads close to the fabric. Use larger fabric scissors for cutting your aida to size.

LIGHT

Always stitch under great lighting. If you're struggling to tell one colour from another or to count dark-coloured stitches, switch a brighter light on! A daylight bulb or lamp is a great investment if you stitch at night. Your eyes will thank you.

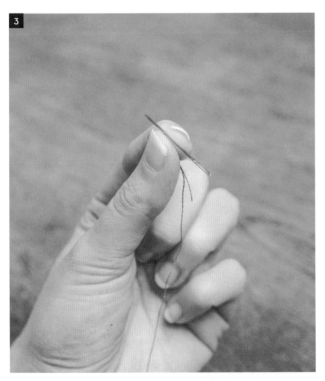

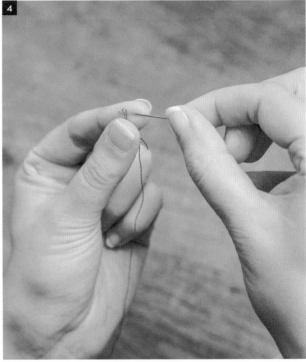

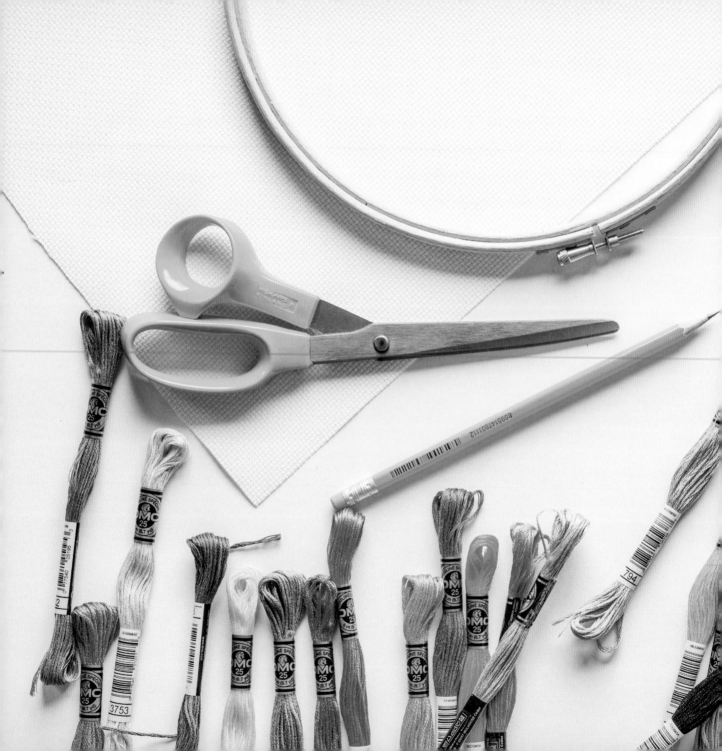

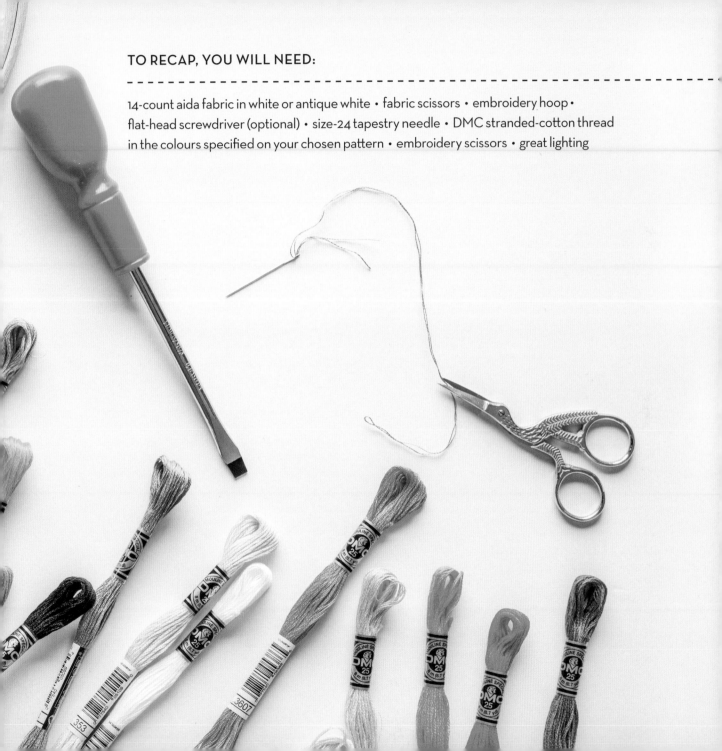

TO RECAP, YOU WILL NEED:

- -

14-count aida fabric in white or antique white • fabric scissors • embroidery hoop•
flat-head screwdriver (optional) • size-24 tapestry needle • DMC stranded-cotton thread
in the colours specified on your chosen pattern • embroidery scissors • great lighting

HOW TO CROSS-STITCH

MAKING A STITCH

A cross-stitch chart is like a map (1). Each grid intersection on the chart indicates a hole on the fabric, and the Xs on the chart show you where to make which cross-stitch. Copying the pattern onto fabric (2) by counting out the stitches like this is called (surprisingly!) counted cross-stitch.

A cross-stitch is simply a stitch in the shape of an X: that's a nice, easy way to think of it if you're feeling overwhelmed! In order to make your X, first stitch a forward-slash from one hole to the hole diagonally across from it (3), then stitch a back-slash on top of it to complete the X shape (4). Voilà! It really is that simple!

In a row of stitches, your Xs should butt together and share holes. You can stitch one X at a time, or, if the row uses the same colour thread, do all the forward-slashes before going back on your row to finish your Xs.

Try to stitch all your crosses in the same direction (forward-slash below, back-slash on top) for a neater finish.

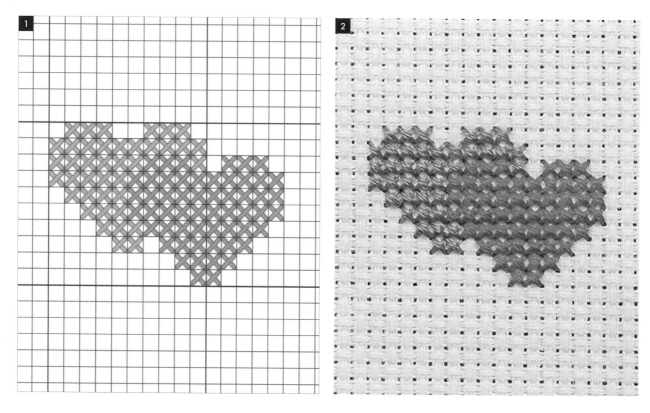

One little miscalculation, an extra stitch or forgotten X can put your entire pattern out, meaning lots of unpicking, swearing and restitching – nightmare! It's harder than you think to keep track of your stitches if you're interrupted halfway through, or keep putting down and picking up your project. To avoid losing count, consider ticking your stitches off the pattern in pencil as you go. Failing that, call it an artistic choice and style it out!

If you need to drag a thread across the back of your work, to carry on with that colour elsewhere, trail the thread across as few stitches as possible. Dark thread will unfortunately show through to the front if you trail it across light stitches, or blank fabric especially, so try to avoid this if you can. Instead, finish your thread and start a new thread, or anchor the trailing thread to your pattern by passing it under existing stitches (5).

You will get the hang of it faster than you think. Remember, a cross-stitch is simply a stitch in the shape of an X!

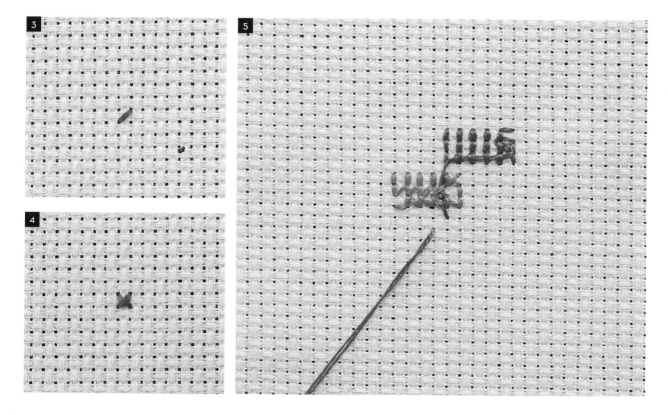

STARTING A STITCH

Start your pattern roughly in the middle of the chart and in the middle of the fabric. That way you'll avoid stitching off the edge. Fold the fabric in four to find the centre.

It's best to stitch without tying knots, to avoid creating bumps that will show up when you frame your work. You want your work to look as neat as possible, so here are two ways of stitching knot-free:

Waste knot

Tie a knot at the end of your thread. Stitch it good-side up, and start your first X a few stitches away (1). Stitch back towards the knot (2), covering the trailing thread at the back to secure it. Snip the knot off, good-side up and close to your stitching. See, it is knot-free now!

Loop

This method only works if you're using an even number of strands, like two strands. Fold your thread in half to create a loop at one end (3). Thread the tail ends into your needle. Keep a hold of the loop at the back (4), as you make your first forward-slash. Now pass the needle through the loop at the back (5) – it will catch and secure the thread as you finish the X.

ENDING A STITCH

Weave your needle under a few stitches on the back to secure it (6). Snip off the excess thread close to your stitching.

If your thread gets twisted as you work, let your needle dangle and untwist naturally.

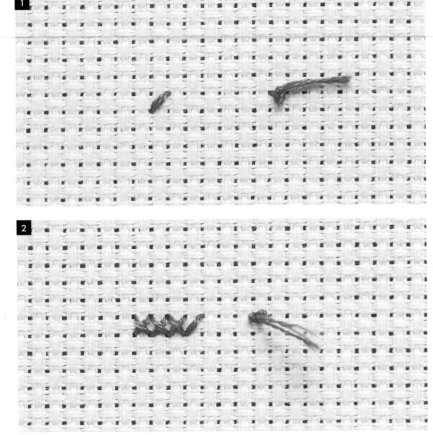

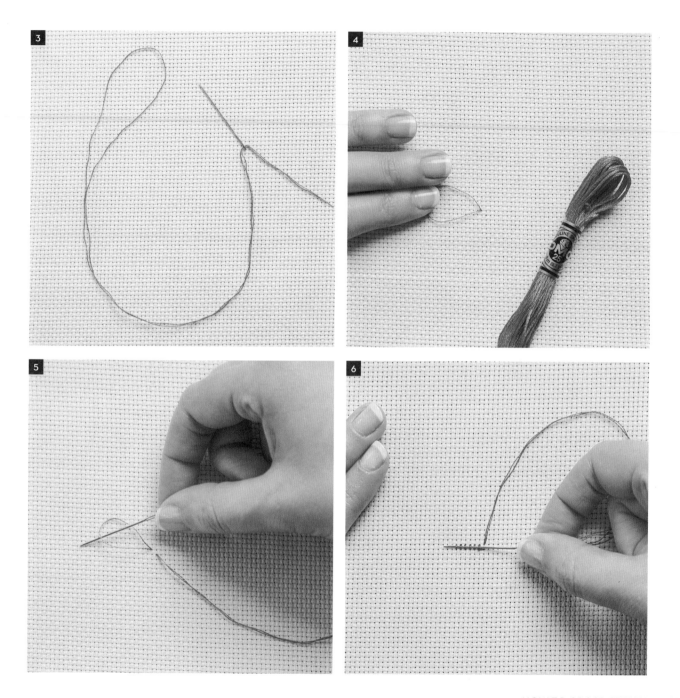

FRAMING YOUR WORK

You will need:

- spray bottle of water
- clean towel
- iron
- frame
- mountboard that fits your frame
- pins
- sharp needle
- strong thread

GET YOUR WORK READY

After all that stitching, you want your masterpiece to look the business when framed – i.e. straight and crease-free. First, dampen your work by spraying it with water. If there are any marks on it, hand-wash it in cold water with gentle (or highly diluted) detergent and rinse well.

To get your handiwork from sopping wet to lightly damp, roll it in a clean towel (1).

Let your work dry flat, gently stretching it back into shape where needed. If creased, place your damp work facedown on to a folded towel. This will avoid crushing your stitches flat or making them look shiny when ironed. Gently iron your work on a medium heat, smoothing it from the middle outwards, until it looks crease-free.

FRAMING YOUR WORK

Pick a nice frame slightly larger than your masterpiece. Cut a piece of mountboard (or ask your local framer to) to fit inside your frame minus 2–3mm to accommodate the fabric.

Place your work face up over the mountboard and reposition it until the stitching looks central.

Fold the fabric over to the back and pin it to the edges of the mountboard, from the middle outwards (2). Keep stretching and pinning the fabric into place, a few centimetres apart. Take your time securing your cross-stitch to the board, until it looks central and taut.

Thread a sharp needle with some strong thread. Fold in the corners of

the fabric, then start lacing together the top and bottom fabric edges, across the back of the mountboard in a zigzag (3). Pull the thread tight to secure your work to the mountboard, before knotting it off. Now neatly fold in the two fabric sides, and lace these together in the same way. Remove the pins.

(If you're feeling super lazy, tape your cross-stitch to the mountboard using masking tape, before unpinning. It'll be our little secret!)

The glass will flatten your stitches if you don't use a spacer inside your frame, which is why cross-stitch is often framed without the glass or in box frames. Go with whatever you prefer.

Now hang that masterpiece up, before inviting your loved ones round for its official unveiling! Don't forget the vol-au-vents.

I GOT 99 PROBLEMS
BUT A STITCH AIN'T ONE

- -

Jay-Z recites a roster of problems in his 2004 single, and any cross-stitcher can relate. Our roll call includes: miscounted stitches, tearing out work that has somehow gone all wonky, dropped needles that disappear into the carpet and reappear in your bare foot, thread all jumbled up in the bottom of your sewing box, grubby fingerprints on your white aida and so on and so on. Now those are problems, Jay-Z, those are problems.

Happily, the problem is also the solution. All that stitching angst can be assuaged with a hoop, a needle and brightly coloured embroidery thread and a few lovely hours to while away the time working on a new pattern. All together now: "I got 99 problems but a stitch ain't one..."

WHY NOT TRY?

Tidying up! It can be oddly soothing to put a work basket in order, and it means the next time you start a project there will be no need to empty the whole thing onto the floor to find an elusive bit of green thread. And that's the best place to start, with those heaps of thread. A handy way to stop them tangling together is to wind each individual shade of thread around its own wooden clothes peg.

DESIGN SIZE

14.3 x 14.3cm | 5.6 x 5.6in | 79 x 79 stitches

LEGEND

310 black

666 red

892 pink

353 peach

SHIT HAPPENS

In French it's *C'est la vie*; in Spanish, *Estas cosas pasan*, and it pretty much means the same thing in any language: bad things happen all the time for no discernible reason. They can be minor niggles or major upheavals, and they head in your direction entirely out of the blue and out of your control. It's much better to acknowledge that there is always going to be something or someone set to ruin your day; fighting against it is only going to make it so much worse. So it's better to take a pre-emptive strike against all that negativity and set yourself the task of cheekily cross-stitching this cheerful little poop. Let's face it, it's tricky not to smile as you stitch, and it's a bit like flipping the bird to a hostile world. It would also make the perfect commiseration gift for a friend who's also weathering the shitstorm that is life.

WHY NOT TRY?

The obvious place to display your completed stitches is in the loo, where, not to be too indelicate about it, shit literally does happen. But you could also hang this in the hallway as a homecoming salute to yourself for having survived the day and its random accumulation of woes, from the inexplicable deletion of important, not-backed-up files to the lid coming off your coffee cup and decanting its contents over your top. It's a little shoulder shrug of a reminder that all that crap is behind you for the time being, and none of it really matters anyway. Tarnished as you are by a general feeling of world weariness, it's probably best to hang it a little lower than head height, as your shoulders will have assumed the slouch position as a natural consequence of having to deal with the day's heap of bull.

DESIGN SIZE

8.4 x 10.9cm | 3.3 x 4.3in | 46 x 60 stitches

LEGEND

310 black
3830 terracotta
B5200 white
3716 pale pink

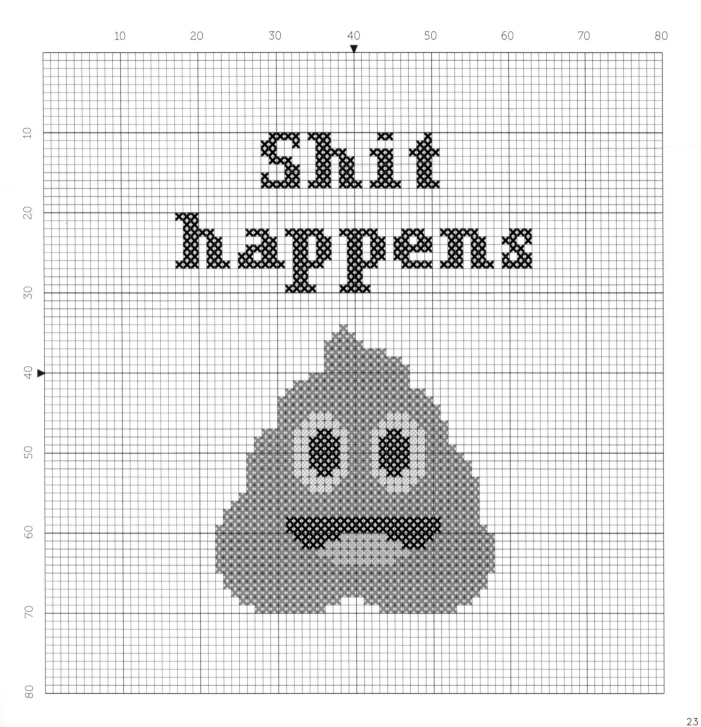

SELFIE-FREE ZONE

- -

While it is usually a happy thing to document the why, when, where and who of your day, there are times and places when selfie Snapchatting and Instagramming all gets a little too much. There are obvious situations when respect, decorum and safety demand you keep your phone in your pocket (funerals, gym changing rooms, cliff edges, window ledges), but there are also everyday incidences when it would be so much better if we stopped posing and paid attention instead. We could have proper chats, appreciate a view, admire a painting in an art gallery. We could get through a whole evening without having to pause while someone else takes a picture of themselves, and we could finish a cross-stitch project without constant self-interruption to take a selfie while stitching. Maybe stash this one in your bag and brandish it at repeat offenders.

WHY NOT TRY?

A selfie zone. It's useless to fight an addiction, so you might as well go for it. Ditch the red halt sign, and embrace full-on digital vanity. It's easy to rejig the pattern to transform it into a selfie zone, just drop the word "free" and eliminate the red warning stitches, and maybe add in a couple of thumbs-up ticks to emphasize that you're snap happy. If you're feeling ambitious, you can ring the changes by surrounding your new message with a frame that takes the shape of a smart phone screen, and cross-stitching in the flash and the camera button. It's a way of paying homage to the technology that has made it so easy to show, not tell, what you're doing.

DESIGN SIZE

5.6 x 8.7cm | 2.2 x 3.4in | 31 x 48 stitches

LEGEND

310 black
666 red
334 blue

WHAT WOULD BEYONCÉ DO?

There are times in life when a luggage load of doubts can threaten to scupper a sense of self-worth. So when you're feeling trapped by a situation that you're unsure how to handle, step back for a moment and ask yourself WWBD? This is the woman whose alter ego is Sasha Fierce; she knows all there is to know about putting the grrr into girl, so the answer is going to be pretty much the same whatever the dilemma. Take control, call the shots and slide any worries to the left. Scared about a job interview? Queen B would just march in like she already works there. BF secretly doing the dirty? In Beyoncé Giselle Knowles-Carter's world, his ass is already kicked to the curb. There is no problem that Bey cannot solve.

WHY NOT TRY?

The best place to put this sampler is the wall opposite your bed, so that it'll be the first thing you see when you wake up in the morning. You could take a picture of it, too, and have it as your screensaver for an extra dash of empowerment when the going gets testing or tough. And it doesn't have to be all about Queen B, you can rework the pattern so that your own chosen hero takes centre stage; step up Taylor Swift, Kamala Khan (aka Ms. Marvel), Hermione Granger. You can swap the crown emblem for something more suitable – a wand for Hermione, cheerleader pom-poms for Tay – and then go all out and make a gallery of stitches with your favourite quotes from your favourite person. Have a look online for more pattern inspirations, and if that sounds like a lot of work, remember, you have the same hours in the day as Beyoncé.

DESIGN SIZE

10.7 x 14.1cm | 4.2 x 5.6in | 59 x 78 stitches

LEGEND

310 black

892 pink

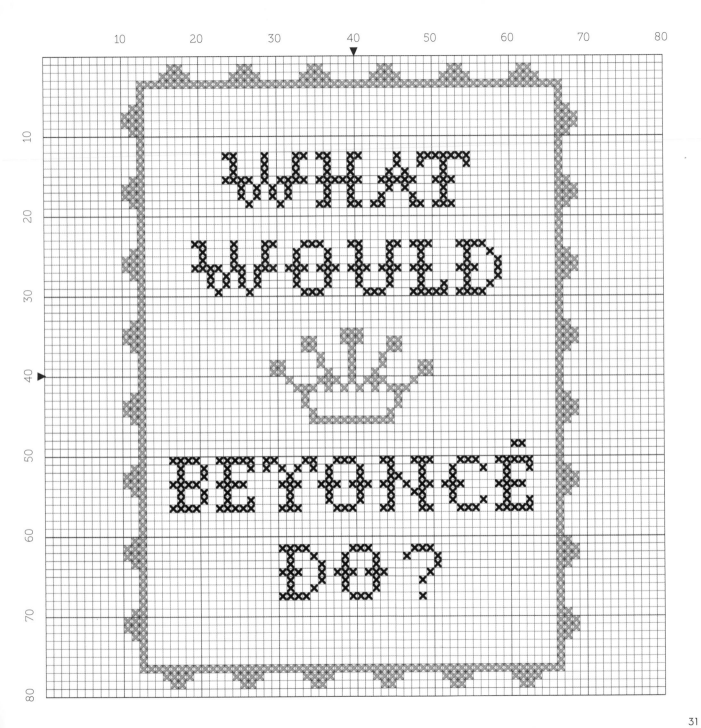

HATERS GONNA HATE

This time-honoured phrase is the perfect snappy comeback to those people who cannot abide to see someone else succeed. Whatever form your accomplishment takes, the haters will feel obliged to crash your happy party with their trash talk. Out in the real world, you could deflect the bile with a blithe "haters gonna hate" (repeated twice for emphasis) as you strut away, with an air of supreme indifference. In the cross-stitch world, coolness, calm and composure – always the best defence – is happily bedecked with rainbows and unicorns and adorned with hearts, the perfect antidote to all that negativity.

Haters gonna hate

WHY NOT TRY?

Make a shrine to your own awesomeness and hang your finished stitch on your wall surrounded by your favourite photos, messages and achievements – from prize certificates to birthday cards, whatever it is that makes you smile.

DESIGN SIZE

6.7 x 13.1cm | 2.6 x 5.1in | 37 x 72 stitches

LEGEND

666 red

608 orange

973 yellow

702 green

3843 blue

794 light blue

3607 plum

310 black

THUG LIFE

Hip hop star Tupac Shakur had this tattooed on his abs (but without the lucky horse-shoe and the garland of pink spring posies – more's the shame), but you don't need to go that far to recognize that you have the resilience to face down whatever mess-with-your-head moments life casts in your path. You might not have to deal with drugs, guns and rival gangs on the morning coffee run, but still there's heartbreak, bossy bosses, your parents coming to stay, your partner's parents coming to stay...the list is endless, and every single item on it is on a mission to make you suffer. It would be easy to be bowed down and broken by the continual assault, but far better to get out your cross-stitch as a reminder that you are more than tough enough to handle whatever thug life pitches in your direction, whether you chose it or not. And you get to say it with flowers.

WHY NOT TRY?

When thug life has done its worst, what you need is a little bit of TLC and some very old-fashioned home comforts. There's nothing like shutting the door on an off-kilter world and snuggling up on the sofa with a fat, billowy cushion that you can nestle into as an antidote to all that aggression. Alternatively, you can work out all that aggro in a more hands-on way, by using a "Thug Life" cushion as a punch-bag. You could niftily sew your stitches onto a cushion you already have or make the whole thing from scratch. The supplies you'll need are basic, and there are tutorials aplenty online.

DESIGN SIZE

12.2 x 12.5cm | 4.8 x 4.9in | 67 x 69 stitches

LEGEND

310 black
702 green
961 dark pink
973 yellow
334 blue

HUGS NOT DRUGS

Tempting as it is to always embrace hedonism as a way of escaping the humdrum, sometimes a hug is the best cure for all manner of ills. A big bear hug, a simple squeeze or a quick cuddle can go a long way to helping you feel a whole lot better. It makes your jittery heart beat slow and steady, it can dispel feelings of loneliness and existential ennui, it dampens down pesky stress hormones, which make you feel weird and wired, while at the same time elevating serotonin and oxytocin – both of which give you a sweet dose of the warm and fuzzies. And there doesn't even have to be another person involved: wrapping your arms round your pet or your old, threadbare ted has exactly the same benefits. You don't have to get high to get happy, hug it out instead.

WHY NOT TRY?

There are times in life, though, when it is all about the drugs. Headaches, hangovers, high temperatures and period pain are all cases in point. Add in coughs and colds and flus and sneezes, hay fever and other minor diseases – there are so many things that can make you feel mopey and life feel miserable. Hundreds and hundreds of years of medical research and pharmaceutical advances mean that you don't have to suffer. So, yeah, a hug might be nice, but paracetamol is necessary. Stitch a "Drugs Not Hugs" for yourself and prop it next to the first-aid box just in case you're tempted to tough it out. And make one for your pregnant friend who is seriously considering natural childbirth; she'll thank you in the end.

DESIGN SIZE

9.6 x 9.6cm | 3.8 x 3.8in | 53 x 53 stitches

LEGEND

310 black
353 peach

SEX, DRUGS & ROCK 'N' ROLL

A slogan that has become shorthand for an old-skool rock 'n' roll way of life. And while some hedonistic-lifestyle seekers take it entirely to heart – like a recipe where no named ingredient should be skimped on – others have a more metaphorical take. It's not necessarily about the sex, the drugs or the music; it's all about the attitude – the more unconventional, devil-may-care the better. This is a message that has pleasure as its mainstay. Put simply, ENJOY YOURSELF is the gist. Whichever way you take it, there's something supremely subversive about celebrating this reckless, rebellious call to ruination in calming, cozy cross-stitch.

WHY NOT TRY?

This is a mantra that you could happily big up. Buy some 6-count binca fabric, which is woven just like aida. Grab a size-22 tapestry needle and stitch up the pattern using the whole six strands of thread – gasp! At 31.8 x 20.7cm (12.5 x 8.2in), your handiwork will be more than double the size. To truly supersize your stitching, photocopy the pattern at way over 100% to be as large as possible. You can use any fabric you want, but for thinner fabrics, add some interfacing to the back according to the packet's instructions. Place the blown-up photocopy, then your fabric, over a lightbox. Trace the Xs onto your fabric using a washable pen, ready for stitching with a large sharp needle and six strands! Once stitched, mount your masterpiece in a suitably fierce frame – bold and brave is the look you're going for.

DESIGN SIZE

13.6 x 8.9cm | 5.4 x 3.5in | 75 x 49 stitches

LEGEND

310 black
666 red
702 green
973 yellow

WALLET? PHONE? KEYS?

It's like a little dance step, with perfectly coordinated moves and its own beat, made by your own fair hands as you pat yourself down to check that life's essentials are all present and correct. And it's a failsafe aide-memoire if you remember to do the moves at the right time. But we're sadly fallible and liable to forget, and it's woefully easy to find yourself on the wrong side of the front door and lacking the wherewithal to go back inside to pick up your phone and wallet. And put your keys in your bag. But if you stitch this and put it at eye level on the front door, all that cursing on the doorstep will be a thing of the past. You'll have done the dance before you've left the house: wallet – check, phone – check, keys – check. You're good to go.

WHY NOT TRY?

Neuroscientists have advocated a common-sense approach to the problem of constantly misplaced items. Over thousands of years our brains have evolved to remember vital information; the only snag is that we're best at remembering things that don't move around much. Wallets, keys and phones are in a permanent state of migration – like unsettled birds, landing on the mantelpiece, down the back of the sofa, on the corner of the kitchen table; they could come to rest anywhere, and it's tricky for the brain to recall their exact location. The easiest way to prevent the daily dither is to award WPKs their own special nesting place – a bowl on the hall table or a neat little shelf all of their own. Then cross out the cross-stitch question marks and replace them with hearty exclamation marks and hang or prop your masterpiece above the new roost. They'll never be lost again.

DESIGN SIZE

13.6 x 10.7cm | 5.4 x 4.2in | 75 x 59 stitches

LEGEND

3843 blue
3845 turquoise

NAMASTE AND SHIT

Namaste is an ancient Sanskrit greeting, which means something like "the spirit in me salutes the spirit in you", and they aren't talking clinking glasses of Jägerbombs and shouting "Cheers!" against a background of dubstep. It comes from a good place, but it's heading in a bad direction. Like Peace Out and YOLO (if you believe in reincarnation or are a cat, the latter doesn't apply to you), it's been co-opted as an open-to-interpretation salute. It can mean that you are one with the universe and really do think there is a divine spark within each of us, or that you think the precise opposite and have a more sarcastic approach to the world. Here's a chance to halt its wayward ways and give it some real definition; adding "and shit" shows that you have fully embraced the second option and are happily heading along a road paved with, er, irony.

WHY NOT TRY?

It would be beyond naughty to make this for your best friend who loves that mind, body, spirit stuff from the bottom of their gentle heart. He or she should be gifted with "Namaste" only and not the other, nasty stuff. Make it for them, put it in a lovely frame and graciously accept their well wishes. Then turn your stitch craft to the bad and make this wickedly snarky version for those meaner individuals who might like the bendy benefits of yoga, but are no way going to admit to embracing any of its other aspects. Just to be on the safe side, get them to prop this far-from-sacred mantra somewhere near their gym kit, as a constant reminder that enlightenment is overrated.

DESIGN SIZE

14.5 x 9.6cm | 5.7 x 3.8in | 80 x 53 stitches

LEGEND

310 black

993 aquamarine

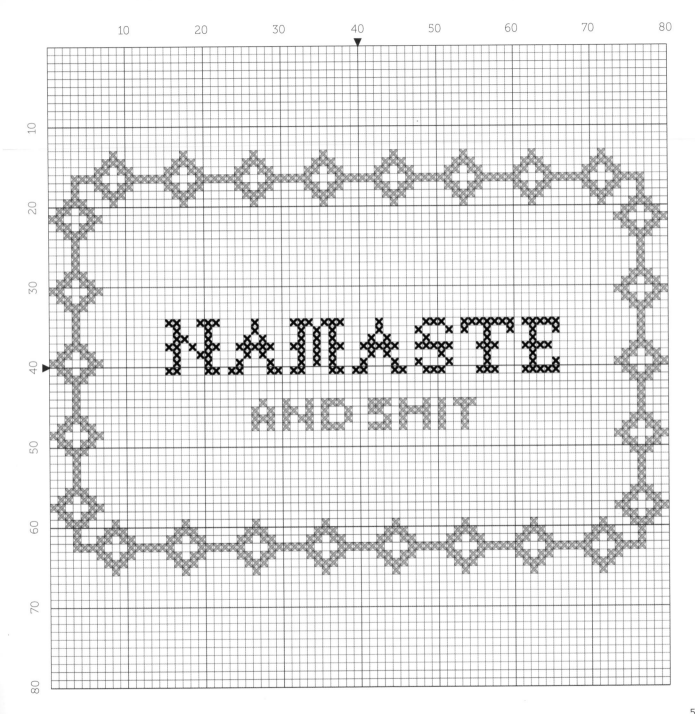

BITCH, PLEASE

Here's a chance to embrace your inner diva. High heels, false eyelashes and the kind of hair that takes you significantly closer to heaven is the attitude you're channelling in these stitches. It's the response for those moments in the day when you cannot believe what your ears (bejewelled with rhinestone drops like chandeliers) are hearing. It could be the obvious lie popping out of someone's mouth, it could be a statement that is so audacious that you cannot suppress your disbelief, or it can take the form of a verbal smackdown to someone who is all over your business and needs to be reprimanded. It's an easy way to dismiss a world of stupidity, too, as well as an all-round excellent comeback to minor annoyances and unreasonable demands – like being asked to load the printer with more paper.

WHY NOT TRY?

It should be no surprise to you that there is actually a nail polish called Bitch, Please!
(It's a metallic pinky purple, in case you're wondering.) It's proof positive that this
is the perfect message for make-up bags. They're easy to make, there are loads of
tutorials online, and they all follow a basic formula.

DESIGN SIZE

14.1 x 11.8cm | 5.6 x 4.6in | 78 x 65 stitches

LEGEND

310 black

892 pink

553 violet

973 yellow

702 green

TO BIEBER OR NOT TO BIEBER? THAT IS THE QUESTION

Shakespeare's *Hamlet*, melancholic, unpredictable and enigmatic, uttered the line "To be, or not to be – that is the question," as he pondered the important matters of love, life and death. Canadian singer Justin Bieber is almost as thoughtful as the Danish prince, and he's certainly as impulsive. He has experimented with his hair, embraced body art and been photographed urinating into a mop bucket in a New York restaurant, among other bits and pieces of general monkey business. Plus he has a "swagger coach" (aka stylist) but still manages to hold sway in the heart of true Beliebers – and plenty of closet Beliebers, too – who would more than appreciate this golden nugget of pop philosophy.

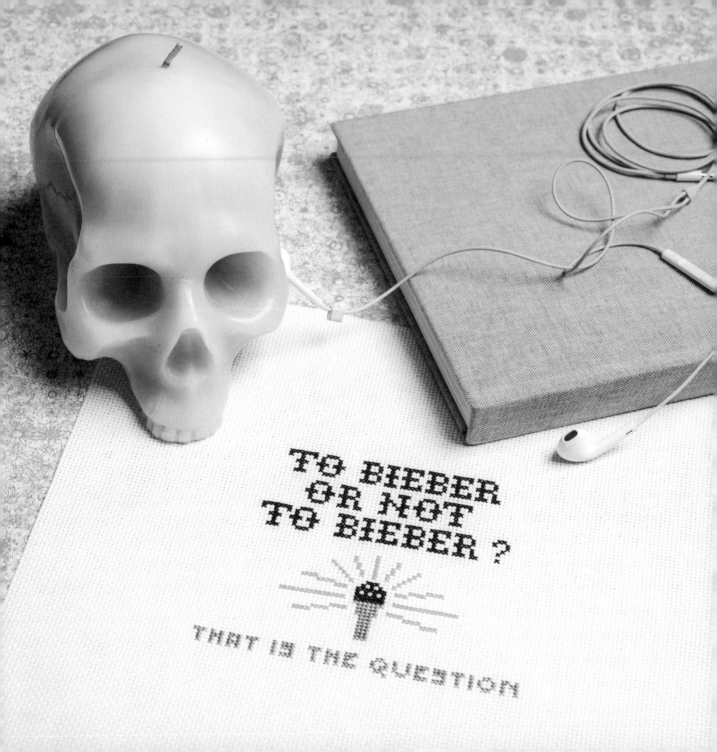

WHY NOT TRY?

If you are handing this over to a Belieber, make their day fantastic by creating a mini-shrine to the singer. First, buy a frame with a large surround. Next, acquire stickers of his quotes and postcards of his poses, learn his favourite colours, download pictures of his tatts, print out a chain of hearts and a string of musical notes, and then assemble a collage that looks like a homage and glue it on the frame. Last but not least, put your stitches in the place of honour. If, however, you're approaching the project more in the spirit of kitsch stitch-up, why not go all out and gild the lily. Trawl junk shops, charity shops and eBay for an antique-style frame decorated with swags, furls and curls – the more elaborate the better. If they're a secret Bieber admirer, then this is a great way to bring their appreciation out into the open.

DESIGN SIZE

13.2 x 11.4cm | 5.2 x 4.5in | 73 x 63 stitches

LEGEND

310 black

973 yellow

169 grey

B5200 white

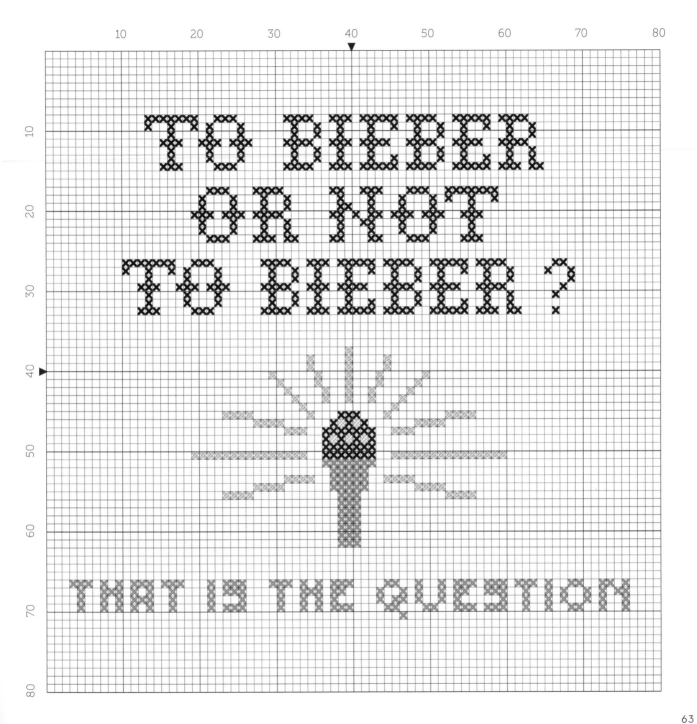

CROSS-STITCH AND CHILL

Oh man, there are times when your day is just a catalogue of disasters, and by the time you get home, you're feeling frazzled, your nerves are in tatters and your stress levels are stratospheric – and the last thing you want is someone sending a booty call under the vague pretence of watching Netflix. Instead, take a deep breath and then get busy with a calming bit of cross-stitching. It is a brilliant stressbuster; you can't worry too much about how your housemates are driving you mad and your landlord won't return your calls if you're focusing on your stitching, and the repetitive action really helps you calm down. There's something very satisfying about creating a finished piece too, and you'll soon find the various stresses of the day slipping away from you as you thread your needle in and out.

WHY NOT TRY?

Making a beginner's cross-stitch kit for a friend who's in the middle of a heap of woes is a lovely way to take their mind off all that strife. Pick an easy pattern chart to start with – maybe one with basic lettering and no elaborate colour decorations to decode – and load up on a few skeins of bright embroidery thread, a tapestry needle and some fabric. Add in an embroidery hoop and a lovely little frame, then package the whole thing up and hand it over.

DESIGN SIZE

14.5 x 13.4cm | 5.7 x 5.3in | 80 x 74 stitches

LEGEND

310 black

993 aquamarine

892 pink

NO SPEAKING
BEFORE COFFEE

It's silly o'clock and you have a dawn chorus of rising friends staying over; they are perky and ready for the day to get started, even without the benefit of a pint of percolated. You, on the other hand, are as grumpy as a grizzly bear who's been roused from hibernation far too early. Tempting as it is to treat them to the full extent of your sleep-deprived irritability, growling at guests is never a good thing. You could attempt conversation, but chances are your surly, short-tempered sentences will not be seen as winsome witticisms or as someone jonesing for a caffeine fix, but incorrectly heard as the incoherent mutterings of a bad-tempered host. Far easier and kinder not to speak at all, and just quietly point to the framed stitches by the espresso machine. Silence, after all, is golden.

WHY NOT TRY?

Your morning coffee mug needs this motto printed on it. If you're feeling crafty you can do it yourself (after you're fully loaded with Java, but not so much that you've got the jitters), but you'll need to lay in some supplies: a plain ceramic mug, a hi-res digital photo of your finished stitches, a printer, water-slide transfer paper and resin sealer. The transfer paper packaging will tell you all you need to know, and there are easy-to-follow step-by-step guides online.

DESIGN SIZE

9.2 x 12.3cm | 3.6 x 4.9in | 51 x 68 stitches

LEGEND

310 black

3753 light blue

334 blue

3858 dark brown

B5200 white

ALPHA AS FUCK

There are many ways to be the leader of the pack – old-fashioned testimony may suggest that an overload of testosterone is the thing to aim for, with a lot of back- slapping and calling people "dude" in a menacing way – but nowadays there are subtler methods of asserting authority. Who needs to be top dog at arm-wrestling when you can wither opponents with the fierceness of your gaze? And you've triumphed at creative cursing – always a winner in situations when being pretty polite just won't cut it. You can say it with words, but you can also say it in cross-stitch. With flowers on.

WHY NOT TRY?

As you've already prettied up this testosterone-fuelled chestbeater with garlands of gorgeous pale pink roses, it would be a shame to miss the opportunity to add a little more flounce to that pastel palette. Head to the haberdashery department and pick out some ribbons in fetching shades. Pop your stitched-up fabric out of the embroidery frame and dab a little bit of glue onto the outer edge of the hoop. Stick the start of the ribbon to the glue and then begin to wrap the ribbon tightly around the hoop, overlapping the layers as you go, so the frame is completely covered. When you're back to where you started, dab another bit of glue on the ribbon to hold everything in place. To hang your hoop on the wall, make a loop with the ribbon and tie it to the screw.

DESIGN SIZE

8.9 x 9.1cm | 3.5 x 3.6in | 49 x 50 stitches

LEGEND

310 black
702 green
904 dark green
961 dark pink
3716 pink
963 light pink

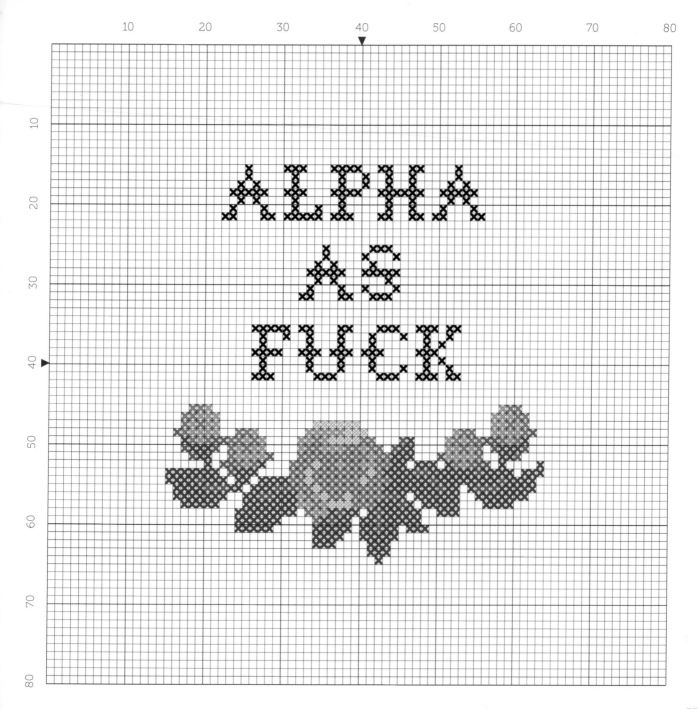

IN TAYLOR WE TRUST

Taylor Swift is "she-mazing". She writes her own music, and her lyrics are about all the stuff that matters – heartbreak, rubbish boyfriends, staying strong in the face of bullies and haters, and being yourself at all times. She's fully prepared to dance (a bit geekily) at awards ceremonies when all the other celebs are sitting there looking solemn and glum (that would be you, Kanye). She has the best girl squad – Selena Gomez, Lorde, Lena Dunham and Jaime King are all her buddies – but is keen on keeping it real by getting out the glitter to make her own homemade cards. She loves her mum, her fans, baking cakes and her cats; Meredith Grey and Olivia Benson are all over her Instagram account. So we're putting our faith in Tay Tay.

WHY NOT TRY?

Using your stitches to make a tote or tee to show that you're Team Taylor. Add some lightweight interfacing to the back of your tee, or if your tote is made of thin fabric. The packet should tell you how. Loosely sew a square of DMC Soluble Canvas to the front. This plasticky canvas is 14-count like the aida used throughout the book, but it will let you cross-stitch directly onto any fabric you want and then magically disappears when dunked in water. Stitch up the pattern as normal and unpick the stitches that are holding the canvas to your tee or tote. Just try not to get any of it wet until you've finished every last cross-stitch! To stop your stitches from itching against you or your treasured possessions, cover the back of your Xs with more interfacing and you're good to go. It would make a great Swift Gift too.

DESIGN SIZE

10 x 12.9cm | 3.9 x 5.1in | 55 x 71 stitches

LEGEND

310 black

553 violet

HAKUNA MATATA MOTHERFUCKER

Way back in 1994, Timon the meerkat and Pumbaa the farty warthog pretty much summed up the slacker way of life in Disney's *The Lion King*. Lion cub Simba's on the run from his troubled past (a wildebeest stampede, a dead dad) and fretful about his future. Enter Timon and Pumbaa, who are all about embracing the present and avoiding untoward responsibilities. Hakuna matata roughly means "no worries" in Swahili, and that's the carefree stance that Pumbaa and Timon aspire to. Add the "motherfucker" to the message, though, and you are in a less laid-back space and more in the territory of *Reservoir Dogs*. Think Samuel L Jackson, with a gun and issues about just about everything. No worries? You should be worried and worse. "Hakuna matata motherfucker" is a perfect mix of snark, snarl and sarcasm, and just the thing to get stitching when you need a more acerbic attitude to life's little problems.

WHY NOT TRY?

This is an essential desk-top ornament. Surrounded as you are by super-sweet co-workers, you will find yourself constantly invited to hippy-happy group activities. A laid-back response is going to get you roped into some horrendous after-work jamboree that involves soul-destroying levels of niceness. This is so not you, so you need these stitches near you to remind yourself that you have a dark heart, dissolute habits and a surly disposition. But how to display it to its best advantage? Surprisingly, now is the time to look toward your eccentric grandma's decorative plate collection (inspiration comes in the strangest places), then get yourself a wire or plastic plate stand and pop your embroidery hoop in. Tempted to agree to a communal campfire sing-along? The HMMF code will make you think again.

DESIGN SIZE

8.1 x 11.1cm | 3.2 x 4.4in | 45 x 61 stitches

LEGEND

310 black

973 yellow

741 orange

608 dark orange

THIS IS MY JAM!

A heartfelt surge of love for your favourite song, expressed in four little words; with an exclamation mark for added enthusiasm and affection. Heavy metal, gangster rap, 60s girl groups, bubble-gum pop, melancholy ballads telling of bad boyfriends, askew tattoos and inevitable heartbreak – anything can be your jam.

WHY NOT TRY?

The sampler would look great on the wall by your record collection, or in your favourite place to cozy up and listen to music. But you can bring the noise out and about with you too with a bit of lo-fi crafting, by making a stitched "This is my jam!" cover for your phone. The easiest way to do it is to get your hands on a "cross-stitch phone case"! It's a real thing – a plastic phone cover that's been perforated to make it cross-stitchable. If you can't find one for your handset, stitch up the wording onto clear plastic canvas instead, cut it to size and fit your sampler into a see-through plastic phone case. It'll even keep your cross-stitches nice and clean – bonus!

DESIGN SIZE

14.3 x 13.6cm | 5.6 x 5.4in | 79 x 75 stitches

LEGEND

798 blue

702 green

973 yellow

892 pink

I'M SORRY FOR WHAT I DID WHEN I WAS HANGRY

Hungry meets angry in a neat little word that describes the effect of low blood sugar on the hot tempered. Snapping, swearing, crashing around like Mark Ruffalo as the Hulk ("Don't make me hangry. You wouldn't like me when I'm hangry") and other grumpy comebacks to ordinary situations look like bad behaviour to your nearest and dearest. But they can be blamed on science and not your appalling character – your brain needs glucose to think rationally; you get glucose from food; no food means plummeting blood-glucose levels, leading your brain to believe that you are in a life-threatening situation, with the added bonus that you don't have enough brain power to stop the snarling. Add in the emergency adrenaline that is cascading into your system and, really, it's no wonder that you're SHOUTING at everyone. Eat something and then apologize in cross-stitch – science can only excuse so much.

WHY NOT TRY?

It could be argued that there's a hollow ring of denial about a hangry apology that comes garnished with images of food. It's a little like you're blaming your favourite snacks for the entire out-of-hand situation in which you're merely an innocent bystander. So express true, heartfelt regret by binning the burger and canning the soft drink, and embellishing your "I'm sorry" with emojis that look like you really mean it. Lots and lots of sad faces. Down-turned mouths. Teardrops flowing like depthless sorrow – there are lots of extra patterns to be found online. Then go get a sandwich.

DESIGN SIZE

12.7 x 12.5cm | 5 x 4.9in | 70 x 69 stitches

LEGEND

310 black
798 blue
976 brown
3858 dark brown
702 green
666 red
973 yellow

I MAKE IT
TEQUILA O'CLOCK

Tick-tock, it's that time of the night when a dash of hard liquor in a shot glass can get the party started, with bad dancing, karaoke and declarations of undying friendship not just to your actual friends but also to random people who have been drawn into the wayward orbit of your merrymaking. The rallying cry for a round of tequilas should be made in a "This is a brilliant idea" tone of voice (even if past experience suggests otherwise), accompanied by brandishing the screenshot of your sampler so everyone gets the message that things are about to get messy. Lay out the lime wedges, sprinkle the salt, pour and let the uproar begin. But remember: get a cab home, and drink some water or your head will feel like a piñata in the morning.

WHY NOT TRY?

Tequila doesn't have to be your cross-stitch go-to drink; it could be vodka, whiskey, or gin, all perfect beverages to create your own minibar at home. Pop your finished sampler into a photo frame. Then find yourself a tray. Assemble an array of pretty glasses on it, with a charity shop cut-glass decanter or cocktail shaker for good measure, and put it all on a shelf or retro sideboard. Add in a salt shaker, garnishes, some of those lovely, silly cocktail umbrellas, a selection of mixers and bottles of your top tipple, and then prop your sampler next to the arrangement for a very stylish set piece. If alcohol isn't your thing, choose thread shades that match (or clash with, for an extra pop of colour) your kitchen and ditch the tequila for tea in the cross-stitch pattern. Frame and hang above the tea caddy.

DESIGN SIZE

10.3 x 13.4cm | 4.1 x 5.3in | 57 x 74 stitches

LEGEND

310 black
169 grey
702 green
973 yellow

ACKNOWLEDGEMENTS

With thanks to Joe at Octopus Publishing for the ridiculously tight deadlines and keeping a straight face when talking about poo; to Jaz, Liz and Max for making cross-stitch ridiculously good-looking; to Eithne and Phoebe for your smooth patter and eagle eyes; to my better half Andrew for tackling the dreaded DIY alone while I worked all the hours; to Bex Smith, Cas Magill, Cathy Pascoe, Claire Brown, Emerald Mosley, Fionna Shilling, Georgie Corke Nieman, Kate Crighton, Lindsay Jakes, Lisa Sparks, Michelle Morley, Nicola Barker, Nicola Davies, Rowena Bayliss and Suzanne Barrett for stitching their hearts out and saving the day!

Keep up the mischief, you magnificent people.

Photo copyright © Lydia Shalet

BIOGRAPHY

Genevieve Brading is the embroiderer behind trendy needlework brand Floss & Mischief. Originally into dressmaking as an antidote to her suited-and-booted corporate job, she launched her needlework company because of an argument about taxidermy! Genevieve's boyfriend wanted to fill the house with very on-trend stuffed and mounted insects, but she put her foot down as it's just too creepy. As a peace offering she designed and stitched some cross-stitch beetles for him.

Floss & Mischief now rocks the taxidermy trend and keeps putting a modern twist on needlework. Genevieve's designs often reference popular culture and passing trends, breathing new life into an old craft. She especially likes small and easy needlework projects, such as the ones in this book, which guarantee quick success and make stitching extra enjoyable.

You'll find Genevieve's work in modern craft shops and haberdasheries across the UK, including Liberty in London. As well as creating her own contemporary cross-stitch kits, she regularly contributes patterns and tutorials to craft magazines.

When Genevieve's not stitching, she's guzzling coffee or arguing with her boyfriend about taxidermy (again). Discover her latest cross-stitch patterns, kits and stitching mischief at **flossandmischief.com**.